easy

Stir-fry

easy

Stir-fry

LOVE FOOD

Love Food ® is an imprint of Parragon Books Ltd

Parragon
Queen Street House
4 Queen Street
Bath BA1 1HE, UK

Designed by Mark Cavanagh
Cover and additional photography by Charlie Richards*
Additional food styling by Mary Wall
Introduction by Anne Sheasby

ISBN: 978-1-4075-2360-6

Printed in China

NOTES FOR THE READER
This book uses imperial, metric, and U.S. cup measurements. Follow the same measurements throughout; do not mix imperial with metric. All spoon measurements are level, unless otherwise stated: teaspoons are assumed to be 5 ml and tablespoons are assumed to be 15 ml. Unless otherwise stated, milk is assumed to be nonfat, eggs and individual vegetables, such as potatoes, are medium, and pepper is freshly ground black pepper. Recipes using raw or very lightly cooked eggs should be avoided by infants, the elderly, pregnant women, convalescents, and anyone with an illness. The times given are an approximate guide only.

*pages 23, 26, 29, 31, 32, 35, 37, 38, 41, 44, 55, 58, 61, 63, 67, 69, 79, 81, 82, 95, 99, 107, 113, 117, 119, 120, 128, 131, 133, 137, 145, 149, 151, 155, and 158.

Contents

Introduction

Stir-frying, and wok cooking in particular, originated mainly from China, but these days it is a familiar method of cooking in many countries all around the world.

Stir-frying is a versatile and popular cooking style and because everything is cooked together in one pan, it appeals to many. For those of us short of time, stir-fries are the perfect way to create a quick, nutritious, and tasty meal, ideal for the family or for sharing with friends. If you don't have much space in your kitchen, stir-frying is a great, easy way to create a delicious dinner, and you will save time on cleaning up too.

The variety and range of stir-fry recipes is extensive, with the vast majority being savory. Red meat, poultry, and seafood are often combined with a reasonably large quantity of mixed vegetables and sometimes noodles or rice, creating the basis for many appetizing and mouthwatering stir-fries.

Woks

During stir-frying, foods are cooked together quickly while being tossed about rapidly in a hot heavy-bottomed skillet or wok—the widely used Chinese cooking pan with one or two handles. A wok is the most important piece of equipment traditionally used to make stir-fries. Woks, which do vary in size, have a familiar rounded-bottom shape with curved (often steep) sides that ensure food can be tossed around the pan and cooked quickly and efficiently in very little oil. This not only means that it is a fast method of cooking, but also healthy because many vitamins and minerals in the foods are also preserved.

A traditional Chinese wok is made of iron or steel, although other types, such as nonstick and stainless steel woks, are also widely available. A new iron or steel wok will need to be seasoned, or proved, before use to prevent it from rusting and to give it a relatively nonstick surface to stop food from sticking during cooking. To do this, follow the instructions provided with the wok.

Other Essential Equipment

A wooden spatula or wok ladle is essential for stirring and moving the food continuously and briskly in the wok. Chopsticks are also sometimes used for this purpose. A slotted or large spoon is useful for lifting cooked food out of the wok, and a rack that fits onto the rim of the wok and holds food during cooking (while other food is being cooked in the wok) may also be helpful.

Preparing Ingredients for Stir-Fries

When making stir-fries, ingredients should always be prepared beforehand, so that when you start cooking they can be added and tossed together at the appropriate stages during cooking. One important factor in wok cookery is this initial preparation of ingredients, and it is the most time-consuming part. All the ingredients should be cut up into small pieces or strips of a reasonably uniform size to ensure even and quick cooking. Any other ingredients, such as oil, sauces, spices, or other seasonings, should be measured out before you begin. It is crucial when stir-frying that all the ingredients for the recipe are prepared and ready at hand before cooking begins.

Types of Oil

With many recipes, the wok is preheated first, then the oil is added and heated until it is hot and sizzling (and sometimes just beginning to smoke, depending on the recipe) before the rest of the ingredients are added. The type of oil used when stir-frying varies but peanut oil is ideal, and corn oil or sunflower oil also work well. Olive oil is not usually recommended for stir-fries because its composition doesn't enable it to reach temperatures as high as peanut or sunflower oil. Sesame seed oil must also be added only at the last minute as flavoring because it burns at high temperatures.

Successful Stir-Frying

The heat used in stir-frying is usually a high, intense heat (depending on the recipe), again contributing to a quick overall cooking time, with many recipes often requiring only just a few minutes cooking. The heat is usually kept reasonably high throughout the cooking period (subject to the individual recipe). Remember the ingredients that need a longer cooking time should be added to the wok first, followed by those that require a shorter cooking time, so always make sure you add the ingredients to the wok in the correct order—recipes should guide you on this.

1

Meat

Soy & Sesame Beef

serves 4

2 tbsp sesame seeds

2 tbsp vegetable oil

1 lb/450 g beef tenderloin, thinly sliced

1 green bell pepper, seeded and thinly sliced

4 cloves garlic, crushed

2 tbsp dry sherry

4 tbsp soy sauce

6 scallions, sliced

cooked noodles, to serve

Heat a large wok or heavy-bottom skillet until it is very hot.

Add the sesame seeds to the wok or skillet and dry-cook, stirring, for 1–2 minutes, or until they just begin to brown. Take the wok off the heat, remove the sesame seeds, and set them aside until required.

Heat the vegetable oil in the wok or skillet. Add the beef and cook for 2–3 minutes, or until sealed on all sides. Then add the sliced bell pepper and crushed garlic to the wok and continue cooking for 2 minutes.

Add the dry sherry and soy sauce to the wok together with the scallions. Allow the mixture to bubble, stirring occasionally, for about 1 minute, but be sure not to let the mixture burn.

Transfer the garlic beef stir-fry to warm serving bowls and scatter with the dry-cooked sesame seeds. Serve hot with freshly cooked noodles.

Marinated Beef with Vegetables

serves 4

for the marinade

1 tbsp dry sherry

½ tbsp soy sauce

½ tbsp cornstarch

½ tsp superfine sugar

2 garlic cloves, finely chopped

1 tbsp sesame oil

for the stir-fry

1 lb 2 oz/500 g sirloin or top round steak, cut into thin strips

3 tbsp peanut oil

½ tbsp cornstarch

½ tbsp soy sauce

1 head of broccoli, cut into florets

2 carrots, cut into thin strips

1¼ cups snow peas

½ cup beef stock

9 oz/250 g baby spinach, shredded

cooked white rice or noodles, to serve

To make the marinade, mix the sherry, soy sauce, cornstarch, sugar, garlic, and sesame oil in a bowl. Add the beef to the mixture, cover with plastic wrap, and let marinate for 30 minutes.

Heat 1 tablespoon of the oil in a wok or skillet. Stir-fry the beef without its marinade for 2 minutes, or until medium-rare. Discard the marinade. Remove the beef from the wok and set aside.

Combine the cornstarch and soy sauce in a bowl and set aside. Pour the remaining 2 tablespoons of peanut oil into the wok, add the broccoli, carrots, and snow peas and stir-fry for 2 minutes.

Add the stock, then cover the pan and steam for one minute. Stir in the spinach, beef, and the cornstarch mixture. Cook until the juices boil and thicken.

Serve over freshly cooked white rice or noodles.

Hot & Spicy Beef with Toasted Pine Nuts

serves 4

for the marinade

2 tbsp soy sauce

1 tbsp cornstarch

1 tbsp water

for the stir-fry

1 lb/450 g sirloin or top round steak, cut into thin strips

⅓ cup pine nuts

juice of 1 lime

1 tbsp soy sauce

2 tbsp white wine vinegar

1 tsp cornstarch

2 tbsp peanut oil

3 tsp grated fresh ginger

2 red, hot chiles, finely chopped

4 small baby leeks, halved

2 carrots, thinly sliced

3½ oz/100 g fine tip asparagus

3 shallots, thinly sliced

cooked noodles, to serve

To make the marinade, mix the soy sauce with the cornstarch and water in a medium bowl. Add the beef and stir until the meat is well coated. Cover the bowl with plastic wrap and chill in the refrigerator for 1 hour. Spread the pine nuts on a baking sheet and toast under a broiler until lightly browned.

Mix the lime juice, soy sauce, vinegar, cornstarch, and 1 tablespoon of the peanut oil in a small bowl and set aside. Heat the remaining peanut oil in a wok or large skillet. Stir-fry the ginger, chiles, and leeks for 2 minutes. Add the beef and the marinade and stir-fry for another minute.

Stir in the carrots, asparagus, and shallots and cook for several minutes, or until the beef is cooked through. Add the lime mixture, then reduce the heat and simmer until the liquid thickens. Remove from the heat and sprinkle with the pine nuts and serve with freshly cooked noodles.

Hot Sesame Beef

1 lb 2 oz/500 g beef tenderloin, cut into thin strips

1½ tbsp sesame seeds

½ cup beef stock

2 tbsp soy sauce

2 tbsp grated fresh ginger

2 garlic cloves, finely chopped

1 tsp cornstarch

½ tsp chile flakes

3 tbsp peanut oil

1 large head of broccoli, cut into florets

1 yellow bell pepper, thinly sliced

1 red chile, seeded and finely sliced

1 tbsp chili oil, to taste

cooked wild rice, to serve

1 tbsp chopped fresh cilantro, to garnish

Mix the beef strips with 1 tablespoon of the sesame seeds in a small bowl. In a separate bowl, whisk together the beef stock, soy sauce, ginger, garlic, cornstarch, and chile flakes.

Heat 1 tablespoon of the peanut oil in a large wok or skillet. Stir-fry the beef strips for 2–3 minutes. Remove and set aside.

Discard any oil remaining in the wok, then wipe with paper towels to remove any stray sesame seeds. Heat the remaining oil and add the broccoli, pepper, chile and chili oil, then stir-fry for 2–3 minutes. Stir in the beef bouillon mixture, then cover and simmer for 2 minutes.

Return the beef to the wok and simmer until the juices thicken, stirring occasionally. Cook for another 1–2 minutes.

Sprinkle with the remaining sesame seeds. Serve over freshly cooked wild rice and garnish with fresh cilantro.

Ginger Beef with Yellow Bell Peppers

serves 4

for the marinade

2 tbsp soy sauce

2 tsp peanut oil

1½ tsp superfine sugar

1 tsp cornstarch

for the stir-fry

1 lb 2 oz/500 g beef
tenderloin, cut into
1-inch/2.5-cm cubes

2 tsp peanut oil

2 garlic cloves, crushed

2 tbsp grated fresh ginger

pinch of chile flakes

2 yellow bell peppers,
thinly sliced

4½ oz/125 g baby corn

1¾ cups snow peas

cooked noodles drizzled
with sesame oil, to serve

To make the marinade, mix the soy sauce, peanut oil, sugar, and cornstarch in a bowl. Stir in the beef cubes, then cover with plastic wrap and set aside to marinate for 30 minutes.

Heat the peanut oil in a wok or skillet over medium heat. Add the garlic, ginger, and chile flakes and cook for 30 seconds. Stir in the yellow bell peppers and baby corn, and stir-fry for 2 minutes. Add the snow peas and cook for another minute.

Remove the vegetables from the wok. Put the beef cubes and marinade into the wok and stir-fry for 3–4 minutes, or until cooked to taste. Return the vegetables to the wok and mix well, then cook until all the ingredients are thoroughly heated through.

Remove from the heat and serve over freshly cooked noodles, drizzled with sesame oil.

Thai Marinated Beef with Celery

serves 4

for the marinade

1 tsp salt

2 tbsp fish sauce

for the stir-fry

1 lb 2 oz/500 g beef tenderloin, cut into thin strips

1 cup vegetable oil

3 celery stalks, cut into 1-inch/2.5-cm thin strips

1 red bell pepper, cut into thin strips

1 red chile, seeds removed, finely sliced

extra fish sauce, to serve

lime quarters, to garnish

To make the marinade, mix the salt and fish sauce in a large bowl and set aside.

Add the beef and toss to coat. Cover with plastic wrap and put in the refrigerator for 1 hour to marinate.

Heat the oil in a wok and deep-fry the beef over medium heat for 2–3 minutes, or until crispy. Remove the wok from the heat and, using a slotted spoon, lift out the meat and drain it on paper towels. Discard all but 2 tablespoons of the oil.

Reheat the remaining oil in the wok and stir-fry the celery, red bell pepper and chile for 1 minute. Add the beef and cook until hot.

Serve with extra fish sauce and garnish with lime.

Stir-Fried Beef with Broccoli & Ginger

serves 4–6

for the marinade

1 tbsp light soy sauce

1 tsp sesame oil

1 tsp Shaoxing rice wine

1 tsp sugar

pinch of white pepper

for the stir-fry

12 oz/350 g beef tenderloin, cut into thin strips

1 head of broccoli, cut into small florets

2 tbsp vegetable or peanut oil

1 garlic clove, finely chopped

1 tsp finely chopped fresh ginger

1 small onion, finely sliced

1 tsp salt

1 tsp light soy sauce

Combine the marinade ingredients in a bowl, then mix in the beef. Cover and leave to stand for 1 hour, basting occasionally. Blanch the broccoli in a large pan of boiling water for 30 seconds. Drain and set aside.

In a preheated wok, heat 1 tablespoon of the oil and stir-fry the garlic, ginger, and onion for 1 minute. Add the broccoli and stir-fry for an additional minute. Remove from the wok and set aside. Wipe the wok clean.

In the clean preheated wok, heat the remaining oil and stir-fry the beef until the color has changed. Return the broccoli mixture to the wok with the salt and light soy sauce and stir until cooked through. Serve immediately.

Beef Chop Suey

serves 4

for the marinade

1 tbsp Shaoxing rice wine

pinch of white pepper

pinch of salt

1 tbsp light soy sauce

½ tsp sesame oil

for the stir-fry

1 lb/450 g sirloin or top round steak, finely sliced

1 head of broccoli, cut into small florets

2 tbsp vegetable or peanut oil

1 onion, finely sliced

2 celery stalks, finely sliced diagonally

2 cups snow peas, sliced in half lengthwise

½ cup fresh or canned bamboo shoots, rinsed and julienned (if using fresh shoots, boil in water first for 30 minutes)

8 water chestnuts, finely sliced

4 cups finely sliced mushrooms

1 tbsp oyster sauce

1 tsp salt

cooked rice, to serve

Combine all the marinade ingredients in a bowl and marinate the beef for at least 20 minutes. Blanch the broccoli in a large pan of boiling water for 30 seconds. Drain and set aside.

In a preheated wok, heat 1 tablespoon of the oil and stir-fry the beef until the color has changed. Remove and set aside. Wipe the wok clean.

In the clean wok, heat the remaining oil and stir-fry the onion for 1 minute. Add the celery and broccoli and cook for 2 minutes. Add the snow peas, bamboo shoots, chestnuts, and mushrooms and cook for 1 minute. Add the beef, then season with the oyster sauce and serve with freshly cooked rice.

Lamb with Satay Sauce

serves 4

1 lb/450 g loin of lamb

1 tbsp mild curry paste

2/3 cup coconut milk

2 cloves garlic, crushed

1/2 tsp chili powder

1/2 tsp cumin

cilantro sprigs, to garnish

for the satay sauce

1 tbsp corn oil

1 onion, diced

6 tbsp crunchy peanut butter

1 tsp tomato paste

1 tsp fresh lime juice

generous 1/3 cup cold water

Using a sharp knife, thinly slice the lamb and place in a large dish.

Mix together the curry paste, coconut milk, garlic, chili powder, and cumin in a bowl. Pour over the lamb, toss well, cover, and marinate for 30 minutes.

To make the satay sauce, heat the oil in a large wok and cook the onion for 5 minutes, then reduce the heat and cook for 5 minutes.

Stir in the peanut butter, tomato paste, lime juice, and water.

Thread the lamb onto wooden skewers, reserving the marinade.

Broil the lamb skewers under a hot broiler for 6–8 minutes, turning once.

Add the reserved marinade to the wok, bring to a boil, and cook for 5 minutes. Serve the lamb skewers with the satay sauce and garnish with the cilantro sprigs.

Lamb with Black Bean Sauce

serves 4

1 lb/450 g lamb neck fillet or boneless leg of lamb

1 egg white, lightly beaten

4 tbsp cornstarch

1 tsp Chinese five-spice powder

3 tbsp sunflower oil

1 red onion, sliced

1 red bell pepper, seeded and sliced

1 green bell pepper, seeded and sliced

1 yellow or orange bell pepper, seeded and sliced

5 tbsp black bean sauce

cooked rice or noodles, to serve

Using a sharp knife, slice the lamb into very thin strips.

Mix together the egg white, cornstarch, and Chinese five-spice powder. Toss the lamb strips in the mixture until evenly coated.

Heat the oil in a wok and cook the lamb over high heat for 5 minutes, or until it crispens around the edges.

Add the onion and bell pepper slices to the wok and cook for 5–6 minutes, or until the vegetables just begin to soften.

Stir the black bean sauce into the mixture in the wok and heat through.

Transfer the lamb and sauce to warm serving plates and serve hot with freshly cooked rice or noodles.

Oyster Sauce Lamb

serves 4

1 lb/450 g lamb leg steaks

1 tsp ground Szechuan
peppercorns

1 tbsp peanut oil

2 cloves garlic, crushed

8 scallions, sliced

2 tbsp dark soy sauce

6 tbsp oyster sauce

2½ cups Napa cabbage,
shredded

shrimp crackers, to serve

Using a sharp knife, remove any excess fat from the lamb.
Slice the lamb thinly.

Sprinkle the ground Szechuan peppercorns over the meat
and toss together until well combined.

Heat the peanut oil in a preheated wok or large heavy-
bottom skillet.

Add the lamb to the wok or skillet and cook for about
5 minutes.

Add the garlic and scallions to the wok, together with the
dark soy sauce, and cook for 2 minutes.

Add the oyster sauce and Napa cabbage and cook for
another 2 minutes, or until the cabbage has wilted and the
juices are bubbling.

Transfer the stir-fry to warm serving bowls and serve hot
with shrimp crackers.

Stir-Fried Lamb with Orange

serves 4

1 lb/450 g ground lamb

2 cloves garlic, crushed

1 tsp cumin seeds

1 tsp ground coriander

1 red onion, sliced

finely grated zest and juice of 1 orange

2 tbsp soy sauce

1 orange, peeled and segmented

salt and pepper

snipped fresh chives, to garnish

Heat a wok or large skillet, without adding any oil.

Add the ground lamb to the wok. Dry-cook the ground lamb for 5 minutes, or until the meat is evenly browned. Drain away any excess fat from the wok.

Add the garlic, cumin seeds, coriander, and red onion to the wok and cook for another 5 minutes.

Stir in the finely grated orange zest and juice and the soy sauce, mixing until thoroughly combined. Cover, reduce the heat, and let simmer, stirring occasionally, for 15 minutes.

Remove the lid, increase the heat, and add the orange segments. Stir to mix.

Season with salt and pepper to taste and heat through for another 2–3 minutes.

Transfer the stir-fry to warm serving plates and garnish with snipped fresh chives. Serve immediately.

Pork & Crab Meatballs

serves 6

8 oz/225 g pork tenderloin, chopped finely

5¾ oz/170 g canned crabmeat, drained

3 scallions, finely chopped

1 garlic clove, finely chopped

1 tsp Thai red curry paste

1 tbsp cornstarch

1 egg white

vegetable or peanut oil, for deep-frying

cooked rice, to serve

for the sauce

1 tbsp vegetable or peanut oil

2 shallots, chopped

1 garlic clove, crushed

2 large fresh red chiles, seeded and chopped

4 scallions, chopped

3 tomatoes, coarsely chopped

Put the pork and crabmeat into a bowl and mix together. Add the scallions, garlic, curry paste, cornstarch, and egg white, and beat well to make a thick paste. With damp hands shape the mixture into walnut-sized balls.

Heat the oil in a wok and deep-fry the balls, in batches, for 3–4 minutes, turning frequently, until golden brown and cooked. Drain on paper towels and keep warm.

To make the sauce, heat the oil in a wok and stir-fry the shallots and garlic for 1–2 minutes. Add the chiles and scallions and stir-fry for 1–2 minutes, then add the tomatoes. Stir together quickly, then spoon the sauce over the pork and crab balls. Serve immediately with freshly cooked rice.

Hoisin Pork with Garlic Noodles

serves 4

9 oz/250 g dried thick Chinese egg noodles, or Chinese whole-wheat egg noodles

1 lb/450 g pork tenderloin, thinly sliced

1 tsp sugar

1 tbsp peanut or corn oil

4 tbsp rice vinegar

4 tbsp white wine vinegar

4 tbsp bottled hoisin sauce

2 scallions, sliced on the diagonal

about 2 tbsp garlic-flavored corn oil

2 large garlic cloves, thinly sliced

chopped fresh cilantro, to garnish

Start by boiling the noodles for 3 minutes, until soft. Alternatively, cook according to the package instructions. Drain well, rinse under cold water to stop the cooking, and drain again, then set aside.

Meanwhile, sprinkle the pork slices with the sugar and use your hands to toss together. Heat a wok over high heat. Add the oil and heat until it shimmers. Add the pork and stir-fry for about 3 minutes, until the pork is cooked through and is no longer pink. Use a slotted spoon to remove the pork from the wok and keep warm. Add both vinegars to the wok and boil until they are reduced to about 5 tablespoons. Pour in the hoisin sauce with the scallions and let bubble until reduced by half. Add to the pork and stir together.

Quickly wipe out the wok and reheat. Add the garlic-flavored oil and heat until it shimmers. Add the garlic slices and stir around for about 30 seconds, until they are golden and crisp, then use a slotted spoon to scoop them out of the wok and set aside.

Add the noodles to the wok and stir them around to warm them through. Divide the noodles between 4 plates, top with the pork and scallion mixture, and sprinkle over the garlic slices and cilantro.

Sweet & Sour Pork

serves 4

⅔ cup vegetable oil, for deep-frying

8 oz/225 g pork tenderloin, cut into ½-inch/1-cm cubes

1 onion, sliced

1 green bell pepper, seeded and sliced

8 oz/225 g pineapple pieces

1 small carrot, cut into thin strips

1 oz/25 g canned bamboo shoots, drained, rinsed, and halved

cooked rice or noodles, to serve

for the batter

scant ¾ cup all-purpose flour

1 tbsp cornstarch

1½ tsp baking powder

1 tbsp vegetable oil

for the sauce

⅔ cup soft light brown sugar

2 tbsp cornstarch

½ cup white wine vinegar

2 garlic cloves, crushed

4 tbsp tomato paste

6 tbsp pineapple juice

To make the batter, sift the all-purpose flour into a mixing bowl, together with the cornstarch and baking powder. Add the vegetable oil and stir in enough water to make a thick, smooth batter (about ¾ cup).

Pour the vegetable oil into a preheated wok and heat until almost smoking.

Dip the cubes of pork into the batter, and cook in the hot oil, in batches, until the pork is cooked through. Remove the pork from the wok with a slotted spoon and drain on paper towels. Set aside and keep the pork pieces warm until they are required.

Drain all but 1 tablespoon of oil from the wok and return it to the heat. Add the onion, bell pepper, pineapple pieces, carrot, and bamboo shoots, and cook for 1–2 minutes. Remove from the wok with a slotted spoon and set aside.

Mix all of the sauce ingredients together and pour into the wok. Bring to a boil, stirring until thickened and clear. Cook for 1 minute, then return the pork and vegetables to the wok. Cook for a further 1–2 minutes, then transfer to a serving plate and serve with freshly cooked rice or noodles.

Szechuan-Style Pork & Bell Pepper

serves 4

for the marinade

1 tbsp soy sauce

pinch of chile flakes

for the stir-fry

1 lb 2 oz/500 g pork tenderloin, cubed

2 tbsp cornstarch

3 tbsp soy sauce

1 tbsp white wine vinegar

1 cup water

2 tbsp peanut oil

2 leeks, sliced thinly

1 red bell pepper, cut into thin strips

1 zucchini, cut into thin strips

1 carrot, cut into thin strips

pinch of salt

cooked wild rice, to serve

To make the marinade, mix the soy sauce and chile flakes in a bowl. Add the pork and toss to coat. Cover with plastic wrap and let stand for 30 minutes.

Combine the cornstarch, soy sauce, and white wine vinegar in a small bowl. Stir in the water gradually, then set aside.

Heat 1 tablespoon of the oil in a wok or skillet. Add the pork and marinade mixture and stir-fry for 2–3 minutes. Remove the pork from the wok with a slotted spoon and set aside.

Heat the remaining oil in the wok, then add the leeks and red bell pepper and stir-fry for 2 minutes. Next, add the zucchini, carrot, and salt and stir-fry for 2 more minutes.

Stir in the pork and the cornstarch mixture and bring to a boil, stirring constantly until the sauce thickens. Remove from the heat.

Serve immediately with freshly cooked wild rice.

Pork with Basil & Lemon Grass

serves 4

for the marinade

1 stalk lemongrass,
sliced finely

2 tbsp fish sauce

4 tbsp fresh basil, shredded

juice of 1 lime

for the stir-fry

12 oz/350 g pork tenderloin,
cubed

2 tbsp peanut oil

5 cups mushrooms, thinly
sliced

1 zucchini, thinly sliced

2 carrots, thinly sliced

4 oz/115 g canned bamboo
shoots

4 oz/115 g canned water
chestnuts, thinly sliced

1 garlic clove, crushed

½ cup chicken stock

wedges of lime, to garnish

cooked basmati rice,
to serve

To make the marinade, mix the lemongrass, fish sauce, basil, and lime juice in a bowl. Stir in the pork and toss well to coat. Cover with plastic wrap and refrigerate for 1–2 hours.

Heat 1 tablespoon of the oil in a wok or skillet over medium heat. Add the meat and the marinade and stir-fry until the pork is browned. Remove from the wok, set aside and keep warm.

Add the remaining 1 tablespoon of oil to the wok and heat. Add all the vegetables and the garlic and stir-fry for about 3 minutes.

Return the pork to the wok and add the chicken stock. Cook for 5 minutes, or until the stock is reduced.

Transfer the stir-fry to warm serving dishes and garnish with wedges of lime. Serve on a bed of basmati rice.

Sweet & Sour Spareribs

serves 4

1 lb/450 g spareribs, cut into bite-sized pieces

vegetable or peanut oil, for deep-frying, plus 1/1/2 tbsp, for stir-frying

1 green bell pepper, coarsely chopped

1 small onion, coarsely chopped

1 small carrot, finely sliced

½ tsp finely chopped garlic

½ tsp finely chopped fresh ginger

3½ oz/100 g pineapple chunks

for the marinade

2 tsp light soy sauce

½ tsp salt

pinch of white pepper

for the sauce

3 tbsp white rice vinegar

2 tbsp sugar

1 tbsp light soy sauce

1 tbsp ketchup

Combine the marinade ingredients in a bowl with the pork and let marinate for at least 20 minutes.

Heat enough oil for deep-frying in a wok or deep-fat fryer until it reaches 350–375°F/180–190°C, or until a cube of bread browns in 30 seconds. Deep-fry the spareribs for 8 minutes. Drain and set aside.

To prepare the sauce, first mix together the vinegar, sugar, light soy sauce, and ketchup. Set aside.

In a preheated wok, heat 1 tablespoon of the oil and stir-fry the bell pepper, onion, and carrot for 2 minutes. Remove and set aside. Wipe the wok clean.

In the clean preheated wok, heat ½ tablespoon oil and stir-fry the garlic and ginger until fragrant. Add the vinegar mixture. Bring back to a boil and add the pineapple chunks. Finally add the spareribs and the bell pepper, onion, and carrot. Stir until warmed through and serve immediately.

2

Poultry

Chicken & Shiitake Mushrooms

serves 4

for the marinade

scant 1 cup white sugar

1 cup soy sauce

1 tsp Chinese five-spice powder

1 cup sweet sherry

for the stir-fry

2 tbsp vegetable oil

1 lb 8 oz/675 g chicken breast, skinned and cut into 1-inch/2.5-cm chunks

1 tsp grated fresh ginger

3 carrots, thinly sliced

2 onions, thinly sliced

¾ cup bean sprouts

4½ cups fresh or dried shiitake mushrooms, thinly sliced

3 tbsp chopped fresh cilantro

cooked noodles, to serve

To make the marinade, combine the sugar, soy sauce, Chinese five-spice powder, and sweet sherry in a bowl. Mix well and set aside.

In a wok or skillet, heat the oil over medium–high heat. Add the chicken and stir-fry for 2 minutes, then add the ginger and cook for 1 minute, stirring continuously. Add the marinade and cook for 2 more minutes.

One at a time add the carrots, onions, bean sprouts, mushrooms, and cilantro. Stir-fry after each addition.

Once the marinade has reduced and is thick, transfer the stir-fry to warm serving bowls. Serve immediately with freshly cooked noodles.

Gingered Chicken with Toasted Sesame Seeds

serves 4

for the marinade

4 tbsp soy sauce

4 tbsp water

for the stir-fry

1 lb 2 oz/500 g chicken breasts, skinned, and cut into strips

2 tbsp peanut oil

1 leek, thinly sliced

1 head of broccoli, cut into small florets

2 carrots, thinly sliced

½ cauliflower, cut into small florets

1 tsp grated fresh ginger

5 tbsp white wine

2 tbsp sesame seeds

1 tbsp cornstarch

1 tbsp water

cooked rice, to serve

To make the marinade, combine the soy sauce with 4 tablespoons of water in a medium-size dish. Toss and coat the chicken strips in the sauce. Cover the dish with plastic wrap and refrigerate for 1 hour.

Remove the chicken from the marinade with a slotted spoon. Heat the oil in a wok or skillet, and stir-fry the chicken and leek until the chicken is browned and the leek is beginning to soften.

Stir in the vegetables, ginger, and wine. Reduce the heat, cover, and simmer for 5 minutes.

Place the sesame seeds on a baking sheet under a hot broiler until lightly toasted. Stir them once to make sure they toast evenly. Set aside to cool.

In a small bowl, combine the cornstarch with the water and whisk until smooth. Gradually add the liquid to the wok, stirring constantly until thickened.

Pile the stir-fry onto a bed of freshly cooked rice, top with the sesame seeds, and serve.

Hot & Spicy Chicken with Peanuts

serves 4

for the marinade

2 tbsp soy sauce

1 tsp chili powder
(or to taste)

for the stir-fry

12 oz/350 g chicken breasts,
skinned and cut into
chunks

4 tbsp peanut oil

1 clove garlic, finely
chopped

1 tsp grated fresh ginger

3 shallots, thinly sliced

1½ cups carrots, thinly
sliced

1 tsp white wine vinegar

pinch of sugar

scant ⅔ cup roasted
peanuts

1 tbsp peanut oil

cooked rice and cilantro
sprigs, to serve

To make the marinade, mix the soy sauce and chili powder in a bowl. Add the chicken chunks and toss to coat. Cover with plastic wrap and refrigerate for 30 minutes.

Heat the oil in a wok or skillet, and stir-fry the chicken until browned and well cooked. Remove from the wok then set aside and keep warm.

If necessary, add a little more oil to the wok, then add the garlic, ginger, shallots, and carrots. Stir-fry for 2–3 minutes.

Return the chicken to the wok and fry until it is warmed through. Add the vinegar, sugar, and peanuts, then stir well and drizzle with the peanut oil.

Serve immediately with freshly cooked rice and cilantro sprigs.

Chicken with Pistachio Nuts

serves 4

¼ cup chicken stock

2 tbsp soy sauce

2 tbsp dry sherry

3 tsp cornstarch

1 egg white, beaten

½ tsp salt

4 tbsp peanut or vegetable oil

1 lb/450 g chicken breast, skinned and cut into strips

8 cups mushrooms (about 1 lb/450 g, thinly sliced

1 head of broccoli, cut into florets

1¼ cups bean sprouts

3½ oz/100 g canned water chestnuts, drained and thinly sliced

generous 1 cup pistachio nuts, plus extra to garnish

cooked rice, to serve

Combine the chicken stock, soy sauce, and sherry with 1 teaspoon of cornstarch. Stir well and set aside.

Combine the egg white, salt, 2 tablespoons of the oil, and the remaining cornstarch. Toss the chicken in the mixture to coat.

In a wok or skillet, heat the remaining oil until hot. Add the chicken in batches and stir-fry until golden. Remove from the wok and drain on paper towels, then set aside and keep the dish warm.

Add more oil to the wok if needed and stir-fry the mushrooms, then add the broccoli and cook for 2–3 minutes.

Return the chicken to the wok and add the bean sprouts, water chestnuts, and pistachio nuts. Stir-fry until all the ingredients are thoroughly warm. Add the chicken stock mixture and cook, stirring continuously, until thickened.

Serve immediately over a bed of rice garnished with the extra pistachios.

Chicken Fried Rice

serves 4

½ tbsp peanut oil

6 shallots, peeled and cut into fourths

1 lb/450 g cooked, cubed chicken meat

3 tbsp soy sauce

2 carrots, diced

1 celery stalk, diced

1 red bell pepper, diced

1½ cups fresh peas

3½ oz/100 g canned corn kernels

3⅔ cups cooked long-grain rice

2 large eggs, scrambled

Heat the oil in a large wok or skillet over a medium heat. Add the shallots and cook until soft, then add the chicken and 2 tablespoons of the soy sauce and stir-fry for 5–6 minutes.

Stir in the carrots, celery, red bell pepper, peas, and corn and stir-fry for another 5 minutes. Add the rice and stir thoroughly.

Finally stir in the scrambled eggs and the remaining tablespoon of soy sauce. Serve immediately.

Chicken with Cashew Nuts

serves 4–6

1 lb/450 g boneless and skinless chicken meat, cut into bite-sized pieces

3 tbsp light soy sauce

1 tsp Shaoxing rice wine

pinch of sugar

½ tsp salt

3 dried Chinese mushrooms, soaked in warm water for 20 minutes

2 tbsp vegetable or peanut oil

4 slices of fresh ginger

1 tsp finely chopped garlic

1 red bell pepper, cut into 1-inch/2.5-cm squares

generous ½ cup cashew nuts, roasted

Marinate the chicken in 2 tablespoons of the light soy sauce, Shaoxing, sugar, and salt for at least 20 minutes.

Squeeze any excess water from the mushrooms and finely slice, discarding any tough stems. Reserve the soaking water for later use.

In a preheated wok, heat 1 tablespoon of the oil. Add the ginger and stir-fry until fragrant. Stir in the chicken and cook for 2 minutes, or until it begins to turn brown. Before the chicken is cooked through, remove and set aside. Wipe the wok clean.

In the clean wok, heat the remaining oil and stir-fry the garlic until fragrant. Add the mushrooms and red bell pepper and stir-fry for 1 minute. Add about 2 tablespoons of the mushroom soaking water and cook for about 2 minutes, or until the water has evaporated.

Return the chicken to the wok, then add the remaining light soy sauce and the cashew nuts and stir-fry for 2 minutes, or until the chicken is cooked through.

Sweet & Sour Chicken

serves 4–6

1 lb/450 g lean chicken meat, cubed

5 tbsp vegetable or peanut oil

½ tsp minced garlic

½ tsp finely chopped fresh ginger

1 green bell pepper, coarsely chopped

1 onion, coarsely chopped

1 carrot, finely sliced

1 tsp sesame oil

1 tbsp finely chopped scallion

for the marinade

2 tsp light soy sauce

1 tsp Shaoxing rice wine

pinch of white pepper

½ tsp salt

dash of sesame oil

for the sauce

8 tbsp rice vinegar

4 tbsp sugar

2 tsp light soy sauce

6 tbsp ketchup

To make the marinade, combine all the marinade ingredients in a bowl and marinate the chicken pieces for at least 20 minutes.

To prepare the sauce, heat the vinegar in a pan and add the sugar, light soy sauce, and ketchup. Stir to dissolve the sugar, then set aside.

In a preheated wok, heat 3 tablespoons of the oil and stir-fry the chicken until it starts to turn golden brown. Remove and set aside. Wipe the wok clean.

In the clean wok, heat the remaining oil and cook the garlic and ginger until fragrant. Add the vegetables and cook for 2 minutes. Add the chicken and cook for 1 minute. Finally add the sauce and sesame oil, then stir in the scallion and serve.

Gong Bau Chicken

serves 4

2 boneless chicken breasts,
with or without skin, cut
into ½-inch/1-cm cubes

1 tbsp vegetable or
peanut oil

10 dried red chiles or more,
to taste, snipped into
2 or 3 pieces

1 tsp Szechuan peppers

3 garlic cloves, finely sliced

1-inch/2.5-cm piece of
fresh ginger, finely sliced

1 tbsp coarsely chopped
scallion, white part only

generous ½ cup peanuts,
roasted

for the marinade

2 tsp light soy sauce

1 tsp Shaoxing rice wine

½ tsp sugar

for the sauce

1 tsp light soy sauce

1 tsp dark soy sauce

1 tsp black Chinese rice
vinegar

a few drops of sesame oil

2 tbsp chicken stock

1 tsp sugar

To make the marinade, combine all the ingredients for the marinade in a bowl and marinate the chicken, covered, for at least 20 minutes. Combine all the ingredients for the sauce and set aside.

In a preheated wok, heat the oil and stir-fry the chiles and peppers until crisp and fragrant. Toss in the chicken pieces. When they begin to turn white, add the garlic, ginger, and scallion. Stir-fry for about 5 minutes, or until the chicken is cooked.

Pour in the sauce, mix together thoroughly, then stir in the peanuts. Serve immediately.

Chicken San Choy Bau

makes 6

1 tbsp vegetable or peanut oil

3½ oz/100 g chicken, finely chopped

1 oz/25 g water chestnuts, finely chopped

1 tsp finely chopped Chinese chives

¼ cup pine nuts, lightly toasted

1 tsp salt

½ tsp white pepper

6 lettuce leaves, washed

3 tsp plum sauce, to serve

In a preheated wok, heat the oil and stir-fry the chicken for 1 minute. Add the water chestnuts and chives and cook for 2 minutes. Add the pine nuts and cook for 1 minute. Add the salt and pepper and stir.

To serve, place a spoonful of the mixture in the center of each lettuce leaf, then top with the plum sauce and fold the lettuce leaf to make a small roll.

Gingered Chicken & Vegetable Salad

serves 4

4 skinless, boneless chicken breasts

4 scallions, chopped

1-inch piece fresh ginger, finely chopped

2 garlic cloves, crushed

2 tbsp vegetable or peanut oil

for the salad

1 tbsp vegetable or peanut oil

1 onion, sliced

2 garlic cloves, chopped

4 oz/115 g baby corn, halved

1½ cups snow peas, halved lengthwise

1 red bell pepper, seeded and sliced

3-inch/7.5-cm piece cucumber, peeled, seeded, and sliced

4 tbsp Thai soy sauce

1 tbsp jaggery or soft light brown sugar

few Thai basil leaves

6 oz/175 g fine egg noodles

Cut the chicken into large cubes, each about 1 inch/2.5 cm. Mix the scallions, ginger, garlic, and oil together in a shallow dish and add the chicken. Cover and let marinate for at least 3 hours. Lift the meat out of the marinade and set aside.

Heat the oil in a wok and cook the onion for 1–2 minutes before adding the rest of the vegetables except the cucumber. Cook for 2–3 minutes, until just tender. Add the cucumber, half the soy sauce, the sugar, and the basil, and mix gently.

Soak the noodles for 2–3 minutes (check the package instructions), or until tender, and drain well. Sprinkle the remaining soy sauce over them and arrange on plates. Top with the cooked vegetables.

Add a little more oil to the wok if necessary and cook the chicken over fairly high heat until browned on all sides. Arrange the chicken cubes on top of the salad and serve hot or warm.

Red Chicken Salad

serves 4

4 boneless chicken breasts

2 tbsp Thai red curry paste

2 tbsp vegetable or peanut oil

1 head Napa cabbage, shredded

1 cup bok choy, torn into large pieces

½ savoy cabbage, shredded

2 shallots, finely chopped

2 garlic cloves, crushed

1 tbsp rice wine vinegar

2 tbsp sweet chili sauce

2 tbsp Thai soy sauce

Score the chicken several times and rub the curry paste into each cut. Cover and let chill overnight.

When ready, cook the chicken in a wok over medium heat for 5–6 minutes, turning once or twice, until cooked through. Keep warm.

Heat 1 tablespoon of the oil in a wok and stir-fry the Napa cabbage, bok choy, and savoy cabbage until just wilted. Add the remaining oil, shallots, and garlic, and stir-fry until just tender but not browned. Add the vinegar, chili sauce, and soy sauce. Remove from the heat.

Arrange the stir-fried leaves on 4 serving plates. Slice the chicken, arrange on top, and drizzle the hot dressing over the dish. Serve immediately.

Yaki Soba

serves 2

14 oz/400 g ramen noodles

1 onion, finely sliced

1⅓ cups bean sprouts

1 red bell pepper, seeded
and finely shredded

about 5½ oz/150 g cooked
chicken breast, sliced

12 cooked shelled shrimp

1 tbsp oil

2 tbsp shoyu (Japanese soy
sauce)

½ tbsp mirin

1 tsp sesame oil

1 tsp roasted sesame seeds

2 scallions, finely sliced

Cook the noodles according to the package instructions, drain well and tip into a bowl.

Mix the onion, bean sprouts, red bell pepper, chicken, and shrimp together in a separate bowl. Stir evenly through the noodles.

Preheat a wok over high heat. Add the oil and heat until very hot. Add the noodle mixture and stir-fry for 4 minutes, or until golden, then add the shoyu, mirin, and sesame oil and toss together.

Divide the mixture between 2 plates, sprinkle with the sesame seeds and scallions, and serve at once.

Turkey, Broccoli & Bok Choi

serves 4

for the marinade

1 tbsp soy sauce

1 tbsp honey

2 cloves garlic, crushed

for the stir-fry

1 lb/450 g turkey breast,
cut into strips

1 tbsp vegetable oil

1 head of broccoli,
cut into florets

2 heads of bok choy, leaves
washed and separated
(or savoy cabbage, if bok
choy is unavailable)

1 red bell pepper, thinly
sliced

¼ cup chicken bouillon

cooked rice, to serve

To make the marinade, combine the soy sauce, honey, and garlic in a medium-size bowl. Add the turkey and toss to coat. Cover the bowl with plastic wrap and marinate in the refrigerator for 2 hours.

Put a wok or large skillet over medium–high heat and add the oil; heat for 1 minute. Add the turkey and stir-fry for 3 minutes, or until the turkey is opaque. Remove with a slotted spoon, then set aside and keep warm.

Add the broccoli, bok choy (or savoy cabbage), and bell pepper to the wok and stir-fry for 2 minutes. Add the bouillon and continue to stir-fry for 2 minutes, or until the vegetables are crisp yet tender.

Return the turkey to the wok and cook briefly to reheat. Serve immediately with freshly cooked rice.

Turkey with Bamboo Shoots & Water Chestnuts

serves 4

for the marinade

4 tbsp sweet sherry

1 tbsp lemon juice

1 tbsp soy sauce

2 tsp grated fresh ginger

1 clove garlic, crushed

for the stir-fry

1 lb/450 g turkey breast, cubed

1 tbsp sesame oil

10 small mushrooms, cut into halves

1 green bell pepper, cut into strips

1 zucchini, thinly sliced

4 scallions, cut into fourths

4 oz/115 g canned bamboo shoots, drained

4 oz/115 g canned sliced water chestnuts, drained

To make the marinade, combine the sherry, lemon juice, soy sauce, ginger, and garlic in a bowl, then add the turkey and stir. Cover the dish with plastic wrap and refrigerate to marinate for 3–4 hours.

In a wok or skillet, add the oil and heat slowly. Remove the turkey from the marinade with a slotted spoon (reserving the marinade) and stir-fry a few pieces at a time until browned. Remove the turkey from the wok and set aside.

Add the mushrooms, green bell pepper, and zucchini to the wok and stir-fry for 3 minutes. Add the scallions and stir-fry for 1 minute more. Add the bamboo shoots and water chestnuts to the wok, then the turkey along with half of the reserved marinade. Stir over medium–high heat for another 2–3 minutes, or until the ingredients are evenly coated and the marinade has reduced.

Serve immediately in warmed bowls.

Lemon Turkey with Spinach

serves 4

for the marinade

1 tbsp soy sauce

1 tbsp white wine vinegar

1 tsp cornstarch

1 tsp finely grated lemon zest

½ tsp finely ground black pepper

for the stir-fry

1 lb/450 g turkey breast, cut into strips

1 tbsp vegetable oil

6 scallions, finely sliced

½ lemon, peeled and thinly sliced

1 garlic clove, finely chopped

10½ oz/300 g spinach, washed, drained, and coarsely chopped

3 tbsp chopped fresh flat-leaf parsley

cooked pasta, to serve

lemon slices, to garnish

sprigs of flat-leaf parsley, to garnish

To make the marinade, put the soy sauce, vinegar, cornstarch, lemon zest, and pepper in a bowl and mix thoroughly. Add the turkey and stir to coat. Cover with plastic wrap and marinate in the refrigerator for 30 minutes.

Heat the oil in a large wok or skillet. Add the turkey and the marinade and cook over medium heat for 2–3 minutes, or until the turkey is opaque.

Add the scallions, lemon slices, and garlic and cook for another 2–3 minutes. Stir in the spinach and parsley and cook until the spinach is just wilted.

Remove from the heat and spoon over freshly cooked pasta and garnish with lemon slices and sprigs of parsley before serving.

Duck with Mixed Bell Peppers

serves 4

1 tbsp vegetable or peanut oil

2 duck breasts, skin on

1 onion, sliced

2 garlic cloves, chopped

1 red bell pepper, seeded and chopped

1 green bell pepper, seeded and chopped

1 yellow bell pepper, seeded and chopped

4 tomatoes, peeled, seeded, and chopped

²⁄₃ cup stock

3 tbsp Thai soy sauce

cooked noodles, garnished with chopped scallion, to serve

Heat the oil in a wok and cook the duck breasts over high heat until crisp and brown. Turn over and cook until cooked through. Lift out and keep warm.

Pour off any excess fat and stir-fry the onion and garlic for 2–3 minutes, until softened and lightly browned.

Add the bell peppers and stir-fry for 2–3 minutes, until tender. Add the tomatoes, stock, and soy sauce, and let simmer for 1–2 minutes. Transfer to a serving plate. Slice the duck thickly and arrange on top, spooning any sauce over it. Serve with freshly cooked noodles garnished with chopped scallion.

Duck Salad

serves 4

4 boneless duck breasts, skin on

1 lemongrass stalk, broken into three and each cut in half lengthwise

3 tbsp vegetable or peanut oil

2 tbsp sesame oil

1 tsp fish sauce

1 fresh green chile, seeded and chopped

2 tbsp Thai red curry paste

½ fresh pineapple, peeled and sliced

3-inch/7.5-cm piece cucumber, peeled, seeded, and sliced

3 tomatoes, cut into wedges

1 onion, thinly sliced

cilantro, to garnish

for the dressing

juice of 1 lemon

2 garlic cloves, crushed

1 tsp jaggery or soft light brown sugar

2 tbsp vegetable or peanut oil

Unwrap the duck and let the skin dry out overnight in the refrigerator.

The following day, slash the skin side 5 or 6 times. Mix the lemongrass, 2 tablespoons of the oil, all the sesame oil, fish sauce, chile, and curry paste together in a shallow dish and place the duck breasts in the mixture. Turn to coat and rub the marinade into the meat. Let chill for 2–3 hours.

Heat the remaining oil in a wok and cook the duck, skin-side down, over medium heat for 3–4 minutes, until the skin is browned and crisp and the meat cooked most of the way through. Turn the breasts over and cook until browned and the meat is cooked to your liking.

Meanwhile, arrange the pineapple, cucumber, tomatoes, and onions on a platter. Mix the dressing ingredients together and pour over the top.

Lift the duck out of the wok and slice thickly. Arrange the duck slices on top of the salad and serve while still hot, and garnish with a few leaves of fresh cilantro.

Fruity Duck Stir-Fry

serves 4

4 duck breasts

1 tsp Chinese five-spice powder

1 tbsp cornstarch

1 tbsp chili oil

8 oz/225 g pearl onions, peeled

2 cloves garlic, crushed

3½ oz/100 g baby corn

1¼ cups canned pineapple chunks, drained

6 scallions, sliced

1 cup bean sprouts

2 tbsp plum sauce

Remove any skin from the duck breasts. Cut the duck into thin slices.

Mix the Chinese five-spice powder and the cornstarch. Toss the duck in the mixture until well coated.

Heat the oil in a preheated wok. Cook the duck for 10 minutes, or until just beginning to crispen around the edges. Remove from the wok and set aside.

Add the onions and garlic to the wok and cook for 5 minutes, or until softened. Add the baby corn and cook for a further 5 minutes. Add the pineapple, scallions, and bean sprouts and cook for 3–4 minutes. Stir in the plum sauce.

Return the cooked duck to the wok and toss until well mixed. Transfer to warm serving dishes and serve hot.

Fish &
Seafood

Monkfish Stir-Fry

serves 4

2 tsp sesame oil

1 lb/450 g monkfish steaks,
cut into 1-inch/2.5-cm
chunks

1 onion, thinly sliced

3 cloves garlic, finely
chopped

1 tsp grated fresh ginger

8 oz/225 g fine-tip
asparagus

3 cups mushrooms,
thinly sliced

2 tbsp soy sauce

1 tbsp lemon juice

lemon wedges, to garnish

cooked noodles, to serve

Heat the oil in a skillet over medium–high heat. Add the fish, onion, garlic, ginger, asparagus, and mushrooms. Stir-fry for 2–3 minutes.

Stir in the soy sauce and lemon juice and cook for another minute. Remove fro m the heat and transfer to warmed serving dishes.

Garnish with lemon wedges and serve immediately on a bed of freshly cooked noodles.

Salmon & Scallops with Cilantro & Lime

serves 4

6 tbsp peanut oil

10 oz/280 g salmon steak, skinned and cut into 2.5-cm/1-inch chunks

8 oz/225 g scallops

3 carrots, thinly sliced

2 celery stalks, cut into 1-inch/2.5-cm pieces

2 yellow bell peppers, thinly sliced

3 cups oyster mushrooms, thinly sliced

1 clove garlic, crushed

6 tbsp chopped fresh cilantro

3 shallots, thinly sliced

2 limes, juiced

1 tsp lime zest

1 tsp dried red pepper flakes

3 tbsp dry sherry

3 tbsp soy sauce

cooked noodles, to serve

In a large wok or skillet, heat the oil over medium heat. Add the salmon and scallops, and stir-fry for 3 minutes. Remove from the wok, then set aside and keep warm.

Add the carrots, celery, bell peppers, mushrooms, and garlic to the wok and stir-fry for 3 minutes. Add the cilantro and shallots, and stir.

Add the lime juice and zest, dried red pepper flakes, sherry, and soy sauce and stir. Return the salmon and scallops to the wok and stir-fry carefully for another minute.

Serve immediately on a bed of freshly cooked noodles.

Fried Fish with Pine Nuts

serves 4–6

½ tsp salt

1 lb/450 g thick white fish fillets, cut into 1-inch/2.5-cm cubes

2 dried Chinese mushrooms, soaked in warm water for 20 minutes

3 tbsp vegetable or peanut oil

1-inch/2.5-cm piece of fresh ginger, finely shredded

1 tbsp chopped scallion

1 red bell pepper, cut into 1-inch/2.5-cm squares

1 green bell pepper, cut into 1-inch/2.5-cm squares

1 oz/25 g fresh or canned bamboo shoots, rinsed and cut into small cubes (if using fresh shoots, boil in water first for 30 minutes)

2 tsp Shaoxing rice wine

2 tbsp pine nuts, toasted

freshly cooked rice, to serve

Sprinkle the salt over the fish and set aside for 20 minutes. Squeeze out any excess water from the mushrooms and finely slice, discarding any tough stems.

In a preheated wok, heat 2 tablespoons of the oil and fry the fish for 3 minutes. Drain the fish, set aside, and then wipe the wok clean.

In the clean, preheated wok, heat the remaining oil and toss in the ginger. Stir until fragrant, then add the scallion, peppers, bamboo shoots, mushrooms, and Shaoxing and cook for 1–2 minutes.

Finally, add the fish and stir to warm through. Sprinkle with pine nuts and serve with freshly cooked rice.

Fish in Coconut

serves 4

2 tbsp vegetable or peanut oil

6 scallions, coarsely chopped

1-inch/2.5-cm piece fresh ginger, grated

2–3 tbsp Thai red curry paste

1¾ cups coconut milk

⅔ cup fish stock

4 kaffir lime leaves

1 lemongrass stalk, broken in half

12 oz/350 g white fish fillets, skinned and cut into chunks

8 oz/225 g squid rings and tentacles

8 oz/225 g large, cooked, peeled shrimp

1 tbsp fish sauce

2 tbsp Thai soy sauce

4 tbsp chopped fresh Chinese chives

cooked jasmine rice with chopped fresh cilantro, to serve

Heat the oil in a wok and stir-fry the scallions and ginger for 1–2 minutes. Add the curry paste and stir-fry for 1–2 minutes.

Add the coconut milk, fish stock, lime leaves, and lemongrass. Bring to a boil, then reduce the heat and let simmer for 1 minute.

Add the fish, squid, and shrimp, and let simmer for 2–3 minutes, until the fish is cooked. Add the fish sauce and soy sauce and stir in the chives. Serve immediately with freshly cooked jasmine rice with fresh cilantro stirred through it.

Spicy Thai Seafood Stew

serves 4

7 oz/200 g squid, cleaned and tentacles discarded

1 lb 2 oz/500 g firm white fish fillet, preferably monkfish or halibut

1 tbsp corn oil

4 shallots, finely chopped

2 garlic cloves, finely chopped

2 tbsp Thai green curry paste

2 small lemongrass stems, finely chopped

1 tsp shrimp paste

generous 2 cups coconut milk

7 oz/200 g raw jumbo shrimp, peeled and deveined

12 live clams in shells, cleaned

8 fresh basil leaves, finely shredded

fresh basil leaves, to garnish

cooked rice, to serve

Using a sharp knife, cut the squid body cavities into thick rings and the white fish into bite-size chunks.

Heat the oil in a large preheated wok. Add the shallots, garlic, and curry paste and stir-fry for 1–2 minutes. Add the lemongrass and shrimp paste, then stir in the coconut milk and bring to a boil.

Reduce the heat until the liquid is simmering gently, then add the squid, white fish, and shrimp to the wok and simmer for 2 minutes.

Add the clams and simmer for an additional 1 minute, or until the clams have opened. Discard any clams that remain closed.

Sprinkle the shredded basil leaves over the stew. Transfer to serving plates, then garnish with whole basil leaves and serve immediately with freshly cooked rice.

Chiles Stuffed with Fish Paste

serves 4–6

8 oz/225 g white fish, ground

2 tbsp lightly beaten egg

4–6 mild large red and green chiles

vegetable or peanut oil, for shallow-frying

2 garlic cloves, finely chopped

½ tsp fermented black beans, rinsed and lightly mashed

1 tbsp light soy sauce

pinch of sugar

1 tbsp water

for the marinade

1 tsp finely chopped fresh ginger

pinch of salt

pinch of white pepper

½ tsp vegetable or peanut oil

To make the marinade, combine all the ingredients in a bowl and marinate the fish for 20 minutes. Add the egg and mix by hand to create a smooth fish paste.

To prepare the chiles, cut in half lengthwise and scoop out the seeds and loose flesh. Cut into bite-size pieces. Spread each piece of chile with about ½ teaspoon of the fish paste.

In a preheated wok, heat plenty of the oil and cook the chile pieces on both sides, until they begin to turn golden brown. Drain the chiles, set aside, and wipe the wok clean.

Heat 1 tablespoon of fresh oil in the clean wok and stir-fry the garlic until aromatic. Stir in the black beans and mix well. Add the light soy sauce and sugar and stir, then add the chile pieces. Add the water, then cover and simmer over a low heat for 5 minutes. Serve immediately.

Five-Willow Fish

serves 4–6

1 whole sea bass or similar, weighing 1–1 lb 8 oz/ 450–675 g, gutted

2 tsp salt

6 tbsp vegetable or peanut oil

2 slices fresh ginger

2 garlic cloves, finely sliced

2 scallions, coarsely chopped

1 green bell pepper, thinly sliced

1 red bell pepper, thinly sliced

1 carrot, finely sliced

½ cup fresh or canned bamboo shoots, rinsed and thinly sliced (if using fresh shoots, boil in water first for 30 minutes)

2 tomatoes, peeled, seeded, and thinly sliced

1 tbsp Shaoxing rice wine

2 tbsp white rice vinegar

1 tbsp light soy sauce

1 tbsp sugar

Clean the fish and dry thoroughly. Score the fish on both sides with deep, diagonal cuts. Press ½ teaspoon of the salt into the skin.

In a preheated wok, heat 4 tablespoons of the oil and cook the fish for about 4 minutes on each side, or until the flesh is soft. Drain, then set aside on a warmed dish and keep warm. Wipe the wok clean.

In the clean preheated wok, heat the remaining oil and stir-fry the ginger, garlic, and scallions until fragrant. Toss in the vegetables with the remaining salt and stir rapidly for 2–3 minutes. Add the remaining ingredients and mix well for 2–3 minutes. Pour the sauce over the fish and serve at once.

Shrimp with Scallions & Straw Mushrooms

serves 4

2 tbsp vegetable or peanut oil

bunch of scallions, chopped

2 garlic cloves, finely chopped

1¼ cups coconut cream

2 tbsp red curry paste

1 cup fish stock

2 tbsp fish sauce

2 tbsp Thai soy sauce

6 sprigs fresh Thai basil

14 oz/400 g canned straw mushrooms, drained

12 oz/350 g large, cooked peeled shrimp

cooked jasmine rice, to serve

Heat the oil in a wok and stir-fry the scallions and garlic for 2–3 minutes. Add the coconut cream, curry paste, and stock and bring just to a boil.

Stir in the fish sauce and soy sauce, then add the basil, mushrooms, and shrimp. Gradually bring to a boil and serve immediately with freshly cooked jasmine rice.

Shrimp Fu Yung

serves 4–6

1 tbsp vegetable or peanut oil

4 oz/115 g raw shrimp, peeled and deveined

4 eggs, lightly beaten

1 tsp salt

pinch of white pepper

2 tbsp finely chopped Chinese chives

In a preheated wok, heat the oil and stir-fry the shrimp until they begin to turn pink.

Season the beaten eggs with the salt and pepper and pour over the shrimp. Stir-fry for 1 minute, then add the chives.

Cook for an additional 4 minutes, stirring all the time, until the eggs are cooked through but still soft in texture, and serve immediately.

Wok-Fried Jumbo Shrimp in Spicy Sauce

serves 4

3 tbsp vegetable or peanut oil

1 lb/450 g raw jumbo shrimp, deveined but unpeeled

2 tsp finely chopped fresh ginger

1 tsp finely chopped garlic

1 tbsp chopped scallion

2 tbsp chili bean sauce

1 tsp Shaoxing rice wine

1 tsp sugar

½ tsp light soy sauce

1–2 tbsp chicken stock

In a preheated wok, heat the oil, then add in the shrimp and stir-fry over high heat for about 4 minutes. Arrange the shrimp on the sides of the wok out of the oil, then add in the ginger and garlic and stir until fragrant. Add the scallion and chili bean sauce. Stir the shrimp into this mixture.

Lower the heat slightly and add the Shaoxing, sugar, light soy sauce, and a little chicken stock. Cover and cook for an additional minute. Serve immediately.

Ginger Shrimp with Oyster Mushrooms

serves 4

⅔ cup chicken stock

2 tsp sesame seeds

3 tsp grated fresh ginger

1 tbsp soy sauce

¼ tsp hot pepper sauce

1 tsp cornstarch

vegetable oil

3 carrots, thinly sliced

7 cups oyster mushrooms, thinly sliced

1 large red bell pepper, thinly sliced

1 lb/450 g large, raw shrimp, peeled and deveined

2 garlic cloves, crushed

cooked rice, to serve

cilantro, to garnish

In a small bowl, stir together the chicken stock, sesame seeds, ginger, soy sauce, hot pepper sauce, and cornstarch until well blended. Set aside.

In a large wok or skillet, heat 2 tablespoons of the oil. Stir-fry the carrots for 3 minutes, then remove from the wok and set aside.

Add 1 tablespoon more oil to the wok and cook the mushrooms for 2 minutes. Remove from the wok and set aside for later use.

Add more oil if needed and stir-fry the bell pepper with the shrimp and garlic for 3 minutes, or until the shrimp turn pink and opaque.

Stir the sauce again and pour it into the wok. Cook until the mixture bubbles, then return the carrots and mushrooms to the wok. Cover and cook for 2 minutes more, or until heated through.

Serve over hot cooked rice and garnish with cilantro.

Shrimp, Snow Peas & Cashew Nuts

serves 4

generous ½ cup dry roasted cashew nuts

3 tbsp peanut oil

4 scallions, slivered

2 celery stalks, thinly sliced

3 carrots, thinly sliced

3½ oz/100 g baby corn, halved

3 cups mushrooms, finely sliced

1 clove of garlic, coarsely chopped

1 lb/450 g raw shrimp, peeled and deveined

1 tsp cornstarch

2 tbsp soy sauce

¼ cup chicken stock

2 cups savoy cabbage, shredded

1¼ cups snow peas

cooked rice, to serve

Put the skillet over medium heat and add the cashew nuts; toast them until they begin to brown. Remove with a slotted spoon and reserve.

Add the oil to the wok and heat. Add the scallions, celery, carrots, and baby corn and cook, stirring occasionally, over medium–hot heat for 3–4 minutes.

Add the mushrooms and cook until they become brown. Mix in the garlic and shrimp, stirring until the shrimp turn pink.

Mix the cornstarch smoothly with the soy sauce and chicken stock. Add the liquid to the shrimp mixture and stir. Then add the savoy cabbage, snow peas, and all but a few of the cashew nuts and cook for 2 minutes.

Garnish with the reserved cashew nuts and serve on a bed of freshly cooked rice.

Scallops in Black Bean Sauce

serves 4

2 tbsp vegetable or peanut oil

1 tsp finely chopped garlic

1 tsp finely chopped fresh ginger

1 tbsp fermented black beans, rinsed and lightly mashed

14 oz/400 g scallops

½ tsp light soy sauce

1 tsp Shaoxing rice wine

1 tsp sugar

3–4 red Thai chiles, finely chopped

1–2 tsp chicken stock

1 tbsp finely chopped scallion

Heat the oil in a preheated wok. Add the garlic and stir, then add the ginger and stir-fry together for about 1 minute, or until fragrant. Mix in the black beans, add the scallops and stir-fry for 1 minute. Add the light soy sauce, Shaoxing, sugar, and chiles.

Lower the heat and simmer for 2 minutes, then add the stock. Finally, add the scallion, then stir and serve.

Simple Stir-Fried Scallops

serves 4

for the sauce

2 tbsp lemon juice

2 tbsp soy sauce

1 tbsp honey

1 tbsp ground fresh ginger

1 tbsp fish sauce, optional

1 clove garlic, peeled and flattened

for the stir-fry

1 lb/450 g scallops

2 tbsp sesame oil

1 tbsp chopped fresh cilantro

1 tbsp chopped flat-leaf parsley

cooked rice noodles, to serve

To make the sauce, combine the lemon juice, soy sauce, honey, ginger, fish sauce, and garlic in a bowl and stir well to dissolve the honey. Add the scallops and toss to coat.

Heat a wok over the highest heat for 3 minutes. Add the oil and heat for 30 seconds.

Add the scallops, with their sauce, and the cilantro and parsley to the wok. Stir constantly, cooking for about 3 minutes (less time if the scallops are smaller).

Serve immediately with freshly cooked rice noodles.

Sweet Chili Squid

serves 4

2 tbsp sesame oil

10 oz/280 g squid, cut into strips

2 red bell peppers, thinly sliced

3 shallots, thinly sliced

1½ cups mushrooms, thinly sliced

1 tbsp dry sherry

4 tbsp soy sauce

1 tsp sugar

1 tsp hot chile flakes, or to taste

1 clove of garlic, crushed

1 tbsp sesame seeds, toasted

1 tsp sesame oil

cooked rice, to serve

Heat 1 tablespoon of oil in a skillet over medium heat. Add the squid and cook for 2 minutes. Remove from the skillet and set aside.

Add the other tablespoon of oil to the skillet and cook the bell peppers and shallots over medium heat for 1 minute. Add the mushrooms and cook for another 2 minutes.

Return the squid to the skillet and add the sherry, soy sauce, sugar, chile flakes, and garlic, stirring thoroughly. Cook for another 2 minutes.

Sprinkle with the toasted sesame seeds, then drizzle over 1 tsp sesame oil and mix. Serve on a bed of freshly cooked rice.

Stir-Fried Squid with Hot Black Bean Sauce

serves 4

1 lb 10 oz/750 g squid, cleaned and tentacles discarded

1 large red bell pepper, seeded

scant 1 cup snow peas

1 head bok choy

1 tbsp corn oil

1 small fresh red bird's-eye chile, chopped

1 garlic clove, finely chopped

1 tsp grated fresh ginger

2 scallions, chopped

for the sauce

3 tbsp black bean sauce

1 tbsp Thai fish sauce

1 tbsp rice wine or dry sherry

1 tbsp dark soy sauce

1 tsp brown sugar

1 tsp cornstarch

1 tbsp water

Cut the squid body cavities into fourths lengthwise. Use the tip of a small, sharp knife to score a diamond pattern into the flesh without cutting all the way through. Pat dry with paper towels.

Cut the bell pepper into long, thin slices. Cut the snow peas in half diagonally. Coarsely shred the bok choy.

To make the sauce, mix the black bean sauce, fish sauce, rice wine, soy sauce, and sugar together in a bowl. Blend the cornstarch with the water and stir into the other ingredients in the bowl. Reserve the mixture until required.

Heat the oil in a preheated wok. Add the chile, garlic, ginger, and scallions and stir-fry for 1 minute. Add the bell pepper slices and stir-fry for 2 minutes.

Add the squid and stir-fry over high heat for an additional 1 minute. Stir in the snow peas and bok choy and stir for an additional 1 minute, or until wilted.

Stir in the sauce ingredients and cook, stirring constantly, for 2 minutes, or until the sauce thickens and clears. Serve immediately on warmed plates.

Stir-Fried Fresh Crab with Ginger

serves 4

3 tbsp vegetable or peanut oil

2 large fresh crabs, cleaned, broken into pieces and legs cracked with a cleaver

1½-inch/3½-cm fresh ginger, julienned

7 scallions, chopped into 2-inch/5-cm lengths

2 tbsp light soy sauce

1 tsp sugar

pinch of white pepper

In a preheated wok, heat 2 tablespoons of the oil and cook the crab over high heat for 3–4 minutes. Remove and set aside. Wipe the wok clean.

In the clean wok, heat the remaining oil, then add the ginger and stir until fragrant. Add the scallions, then stir in the crab pieces. Add the light soy sauce, sugar, and pepper. Cover and simmer for 1 minute and serve immediately in warmed bowls.

Clams In Black Bean Sauce

serves 4

2 lb/900 g small clams

1 tbsp vegetable or peanut oil

1 tsp finely chopped fresh ginger

1 tsp finely chopped garlic

1 tbsp fermented black beans, rinsed and coarsely chopped

2 tsp Shaoxing rice wine

1 tbsp finely chopped scallion

1 tsp salt (optional)

Start by washing the clams thoroughly. Then let the clams soak in clean water until it is time to drain them and toss them in the wok. Discard any that remain open after soaking.

In a preheated wok, heat the oil and stir-fry the ginger and garlic until fragrant. Add the black beans and cook for 1 minute.

Over a high heat, add the clams and Shaoxing and stir-fry for 2 minutes to mix everything together. Cover and cook for about 3 minutes. Discard any clams that remain closed. Add the scallion and salt, if necessary, and serve immediately.

4

Vegetables

Classic Stir-Fried Vegetables

serves 4

3 tbsp peanut oil

8 scallions, chopped finely

1 garlic clove, crushed

1 tbsp grated fresh ginger

1 head of broccoli, cut into florets

1 orange or yellow bell pepper, coarsely chopped

1½ cups red cabbage, shredded

4½ oz/125 g baby corn

3 cups portobello or 1 generous cup mushrooms, sliced thinly

2¾ cups fresh bean sprouts

9 oz/250 g canned water chestnuts, drained

4 tsp soy sauce

cooked wild rice, to serve

Heat 2 tablespoons of the oil in a large wok over high heat. Stir-fry 6 of the scallions with the garlic and ginger for 30 seconds.

Add the broccoli, bell pepper, and red cabbage and stir-fry for 1–2 minutes. Mix in the baby corn and mushrooms and stir-fry for another 1–2 minutes.

Finally, add the bean sprouts and water chestnuts and cook for another 2 minutes. Pour in the soy sauce to taste and stir well.

Transfer to warm dishes and serve immediately over freshly cooked wild rice, and garnish with the remaining scallions.

Sweet & Sour Vegetables with Cashew

serves 4

1 tbsp vegetable or peanut oil

1 tsp chili oil

2 onions, sliced

2 carrots, thinly sliced

2 zucchini, thinly sliced

1 small head of broccoli, cut into small florets

2¼ cups white mushrooms, sliced

4 oz/115 g small bok choy, halved

2 tbsp jaggery or soft light brown sugar

2 tbsp Thai soy sauce

1 tbsp rice vinegar

scant ½ cup cashews

Heat the oils in a wok and stir-fry the onions for 1–2 minutes, until they start to soften.

Add the carrots, zucchini, and broccoli, and stir-fry for 2–3 minutes. Add the mushrooms, bok choy, sugar, soy sauce, and rice vinegar, and stir-fry for 1–2 minutes.

Meanwhile, dry-fry or toast the cashews. Sprinkle the cashews over the stir-fry and serve immediately.

Spicy Green Beans

serves 4

generous 1¼ cups green beans, trimmed and cut diagonally into 3–4 pieces

2 tbsp vegetable or peanut oil

4 dried chiles, cut into 2 or 3 pieces

½ tsp Szechuan peppers

1 garlic clove, finely sliced

6 thin slices of fresh ginger

2 scallions, white part only, cut diagonally into thin pieces

pinch of sea salt

Blanch the beans in a large pan of boiling water for 30 seconds. Drain and set aside.

In a preheated wok, heat 1 tablespoon of the oil. Over low heat, stir-fry the beans for about 5 minutes, or until they are beginning to wrinkle. Remove and set aside.

Add the remaining oil and stir-fry the chiles and peppers until they are fragrant. Add the garlic, ginger, and scallions and stir-fry until they begin to soften. Add the beans and toss to mix, then add the sea salt and serve immediately on warmed plates.

Oyster Mushrooms & Vegetables with Peanut Chili Sauce

serves 4

1 tbsp vegetable or peanut oil

4 scallions, finely sliced

1 carrot, cut into thin strips

1 zucchini, cut into thin strips

½ head of broccoli, cut into florets

9 cups oyster mushrooms, thinly sliced

2 tbsp crunchy peanut butter

1 tsp chili powder, or to taste

3 tbsp water

cooked rice or noodles, to serve

wedges of lime, to garnish

Heat the oil in a wok until almost smoking. Stir-fry the scallions for 1 minute. Add the carrot and zucchini and stir-fry for another minute. Then add the broccoli and cook for one more minute.

Stir in the mushrooms and cook until they are soft and at least half the liquid they produce has evaporated. Add the peanut butter and stir well. Season with the chili powder to taste. Finally, add the water and cook for one more minute.

Serve over freshly cooked rice or noodles and garnish with wedges of lime.

Stir-Fried Yard-Long Beans with Red Bell Pepper

serves 4–6

10 oz/280 g yard-long beans, cut into 2½-inch/6-cm lengths

1 tbsp vegetable or peanut oil

1 red bell pepper, slivered

pinch of salt

pinch of sugar

Blanch the beans in a large pan of boiling water for 30 seconds. Drain and set aside.

In a preheated wok, heat the oil and stir-fry the beans for 1 minute over high heat. Add the pepper and stir-fry for 1 more minute. Sprinkle the salt and sugar on top and serve.

Stir-Fried Chinese Greens

serves 4

1 tbsp vegetable or peanut oil

1 tsp finely chopped garlic

3 cups leafy Chinese greens, coarsely chopped

½ tsp salt

In a preheated wok, heat the oil and stir-fry the garlic until fragrant. Over high heat, toss in the Chinese greens and salt and stir-fry for 1 minute maximum. Serve immediately.

Stir-Fried Japanese Noodles

serves 4

8 oz/225 g Japanese egg noodles

2 tbsp corn oil

1 red onion, sliced

1 garlic clove, crushed

8 cups mixed mushrooms, such as shiitake, oyster, and cremini

12 oz/350 g bok choy

2 tbsp sweet sherry

6 tbsp soy sauce

4 scallions, sliced

1 tbsp sesame seeds, toasted

Place the noodles in a large bowl, pour over enough boiling water to cover, and let soak for 10 minutes.

Heat the oil in a large, preheated wok. Add the red onion and garlic to the wok and stir-fry for 2–3 minutes, or until softened. Add the mushrooms to the wok and stir-fry for 5 minutes, or until softened. Drain the noodles and add to the wok.

Add the bok choy, sweet sherry, and soy sauce to the wok and toss to mix thoroughly. Stir-fry for 2–3 minutes, or until the liquid is just bubbling. Transfer the noodle mixture to warmed serving bowls, sprinkle with sliced scallions and toasted sesame seeds, and serve immediately.

Egg-Fried Rice

serves 4

2 tbsp vegetable or
peanut oil

2½ cups cooked rice,
chilled

1 egg, well beaten

Heat the oil in a preheated wok and stir-fry the rice for
1 minute, breaking it down as much as possible into
individual grains.

Quickly add the egg, stirring, to coat each piece of rice. Stir
until the egg is cooked and the rice, as much as possible, is
in single grains. Serve immediately.

Spicy Tofu

serves 4

for the marinade

2½ fl oz/75 ml vegetable stock

⅓ cup cornstarch

2 tbsp soy sauce

1 tbsp superfine sugar

pinch of chile flakes

for the stir-fry

9 oz/250 g firm tofu, rinsed and drained thoroughly and cut into ½-inch/1-cm cubes

4 tbsp peanut oil

1 tbsp grated fresh ginger

3 garlic cloves, crushed

4 scallions, thinly sliced

1 head of broccoli, cut into florets

1 carrot, cut into thin strips

1 yellow bell pepper, thinly sliced

5 cups shiitake mushrooms, sliced thinly

steamed rice, to serve

To make the marinade, blend the vegetable stock, cornstarch, soy sauce, sugar, and chile flakes together in a large bowl. Add the tofu and toss well to coat. Set aside to marinate for 20 minutes.

In a wok or large skillet, heat 2 tablespoons of the peanut oil and stir-fry the tofu with its marinade until brown and crispy. Remove from the wok and set aside.

Heat the remaining 2 tablespoons of peanut oil in the wok and stir-fry the ginger, garlic, and scallions for 30 seconds. Add the broccoli, carrot, yellow bell pepper, and mushrooms to the wok and cook for 5–6 minutes. Return the tofu to the wok and stir-fry to reheat. Serve immediately over freshly steamed rice.

Stir-Fried Broccoli

serves 4

2 tbsp vegetable oil

2 medium heads of broccoli, cut into florets

2 tbsp soy sauce

1 tsp cornstarch

1 tbsp superfine sugar

1 tsp grated fresh ginger

1 garlic clove, crushed

pinch of hot chile flakes

1 tsp toasted sesame seeds, to garnish

In a large wok, heat the oil until almost smoking. Stir-fry the broccoli for 4–5 minutes.

In a small bowl, combine the soy sauce, cornstarch, sugar, ginger, garlic, and hot chile flakes. Add the mixture to the broccoli. Cook over low heat, stirring constantly, for 2–3 minutes, until the sauce thickens slightly.

Transfer to a serving dish, then garnish with the sesame seeds and serve immediately.

Spicy Vegetarian Stir-Fry

serves 4

3 tbsp vegetable oil

½ tsp turmeric

1–2 potatoes about 8 oz/225 g potatoes, cut into ½-inch/1-cm dice

3 shallots, chopped finely

1 bay leaf

½ tsp ground cumin

1 tsp finely grated fresh ginger

¼ tsp chili powder

4 tomatoes, coarsely chopped

10½ oz/300 g spinach (trimmed), coarsely chopped

1¼ cups fresh or frozen peas

1 tbsp lemon juice

salt and pepper

cooked basmati rice, to serve

In a wok, heat 2 tablespoons of the oil and add the turmeric and a pinch of salt. Carefully add the potatoes, stirring continuously to coat in the turmeric. Stir-fry for 5 minutes, then remove from the wok and set aside.

Heat the remaining tablespoon of oil and stir-fry the shallots for 1–2 minutes. Mix in the bay leaf, cumin, ginger, and chili powder, then add the tomatoes and stir-fry for 2 minutes.

Add the spinach, mixing well to combine all the flavors. Cover and simmer for 2–3 minutes. Return the potatoes to the wok and add the peas and lemon juice. Cook for 5 minutes, or until the potatoes are tender.

Remove the wok from the heat and discard the bay leaf, then season with salt and pepper. Serve with freshly cooked basmati rice.

Julienne Vegetable Salad

serves 4

4 tbsp vegetable or peanut oil

8 oz/225 g tofu with herbs, cubed

1 red onion, sliced

4 scallions, cut into 2-inch/5-cm lengths

1 garlic clove, chopped

2 carrots, cut into short thin sticks

¾ cup fine green beans, trimmed

1 yellow bell pepper, seeded and cut into strips

1 small head of broccoli, cut into florets

1 large zucchini, cut into short thin sticks

½ cup bean sprouts

2 tbsp red curry paste

4 tbsp Thai soy sauce

1 tbsp rice wine vinegar

1 tsp jaggery or soft, light brown sugar

a few Thai basil leaves

12 oz/350 g rice vermicelli noodles

Heat the oil in a wok or large skillet and cook the tofu cubes for 3–4 minutes, until browned on all sides. Lift out of the oil and drain on paper towels.

Add the onions, scallions, garlic, and carrots to the hot oil and cook for 1–2 minutes before adding the rest of the vegetables, except for the bean sprouts. Stir-fry for 2–3 minutes. Add the bean sprouts, then stir in the curry paste, soy, vinegar, sugar, and basil leaves. Cook for 30 seconds.

Soak the noodles in boiling water or stock for 2–3 minutes (check the package instructions) or until tender and drain well. Arrange the freshly cooked noodles in a warmed bowl.

Pile the vegetables onto the noodles, and serve topped with the tofu cubes. Garnish with extra basil if liked.

Broccoli & Snow Pea Stir-Fry

serves 4

2 tbsp vegetable or peanut oil

dash of sesame oil

1 garlic clove, finely chopped

1½ cups small broccoli florets

1 cup snow peas, trimmed

3 cups Chinese cabbage, chopped into ½-inch/ 1-cm slices

5–6 scallions, finely chopped

½ tsp salt

2 tbsp light soy sauce

1 tbsp Shaoxing rice wine

1 tsp sesame seeds, lightly toasted

In a preheated wok, heat the oils, then add the garlic and stir-fry vigorously. Add all the vegetables and salt and stir-fry over high heat, tossing rapidly, for about 3 minutes.

Pour in the light soy sauce and Shaoxing and cook for an additional 2 minutes. Sprinkle with the sesame seeds and serve hot.

Cauliflower & Beans with Cashew Nuts

serves 4

1 tbsp vegetable or peanut oil

1 tbsp chili oil

1 onion, chopped

2 garlic cloves, chopped

2 tbsp Thai red curry paste

1 small cauliflower, cut into florets

6 oz/175 g yard-long beans, cut into 3-inch/7.5-cm lengths

²/₃ cup vegetable stock

2 tbsp Thai soy sauce

scant ¹/₃ cup toasted cashews, to garnish

Heat both the oils in a wok and stir-fry the onion and garlic until softened. Add the curry paste and stir-fry for 1–2 minutes.

Add the cauliflower and beans and stir-fry for 3–4 minutes, until softened. Pour in the stock and soy sauce and let simmer for 1–2 minutes. Serve immediately, garnished with the cashews.

Hot & Sour Cabbage

serves 4

1 lb/450 g firm white cabbage

1 tbsp vegetable or peanut oil

10 Szechuan peppers or more, to taste

3 dried chiles, coarsely chopped

½ tsp salt

1 tsp white rice vinegar

dash of sesame oil

pinch of sugar

To prepare the cabbage, discard the outer leaves and tough stems. Chop the cabbage into 1¼-inch/ 3-cm squares, breaking up the chunks. Rinse thoroughly in cold water.

In a preheated wok, heat the oil and cook the peppers until fragrant. Stir in the chiles. Add the cabbage, a little at a time, together with the salt, and stir-fry for 2 minutes.

Add the vinegar, sesame oil, and sugar and cook for an additional minute, or until the cabbage is tender. Serve immediately on warmed plates.

Mixed Vegetables with Quick-Fried Basil

serves 4

2 tbsp vegetable or peanut oil

2 garlic cloves, chopped

1 onion, sliced

4 oz/115 g baby corn, cut in half diagonally

½ cucumber, peeled, halved, seeded, and sliced

8 oz/225 g canned water chestnuts, drained and rinsed

¾ cup snow peas, trimmed

2 cups shiitake mushrooms, halved

1 red bell pepper, seeded and thinly sliced

1 tbsp jaggery or soft light brown sugar

2 tbsp Thai soy sauce

1 tbsp fish sauce

1 tbsp rice vinegar

vegetable or peanut oil, for cooking

8–12 sprigs fresh Thai basil

cooked rice, to serve

Heat the oil in a wok and stir-fry the garlic and onion for 1–2 minutes. Add the corn, cucumber, water chestnuts, snow peas, mushrooms, and red bell pepper, and stir-fry for 2–3 minutes, until starting to soften.

Add the sugar, soy sauce, fish sauce, and vinegar, and gradually bring to a boil. Let simmer for 1–2 minutes.

Meanwhile, heat the oil for the basil in a wok and, when hot, add the basil sprigs. Cook for 20–30 seconds, until crisp. Remove with a slotted spoon and drain on paper towels.

Garnish the vegetable stir-fry with the crispy basil and serve immediately with freshly cooked rice.

Stir-Fried Asparagus & Oyster Mushrooms

serves 4

1 lb 2 oz/500 g asparagus, cut into 1-inch/2.5-cm pieces

½ cup chicken stock

1 tbsp cornstarch

1 tbsp water

2 tbsp vegetable oil

5 cups oyster mushrooms, sliced thinly

pinch of chile flakes

salt and pepper, to taste

to garnish

1 tbsp chopped fresh parsley

1 tsp chopped fresh chives

Steam the asparagus for 4–6 minutes, until tender and set aside. Combine the chicken stock, cornstarch, and water in a small bowl and set aside.

Heat the oil in a wok or large skillet over medium heat. Stir-fry the asparagus, mushrooms, and chile flakes for 1–2 minutes. Reduce the heat, add the cornstarch mixture and cook, stirring constantly for 2–3 minutes, or until thick.

Remove from the heat. Season to taste, then garnish with the parsley and chives and serve immediately.

Eggplant with Miso

serves 4

2 eggplants

peanut oil, for stir-frying

1 fresh red chile, sliced

2 tbsp sake

4 tbsp mirin

2 tbsp shoyu (Japanese soy sauce)

3 tbsp hatcho miso

2 tbsp water

Cut the eggplants into wedges.

Preheat a wok over high heat. Add a little oil and heat until very hot. Stir-fry the eggplant, in batches, for 4 minutes, or until browned and cooked through. Add more oil for each batch, if necessary.

Return all the eggplant to the wok together with the chile and stir together. Add the remaining ingredients and toss everything together. Cook, stirring, until the sauce thickens. Serve immediately.